Questions and Answers About
SEASHORE
ANIMALS

MICHAEL CHINERY
ILLUSTRATED BY WAYNE FORD, MICK LOATES, AND MYKE TAYLOR

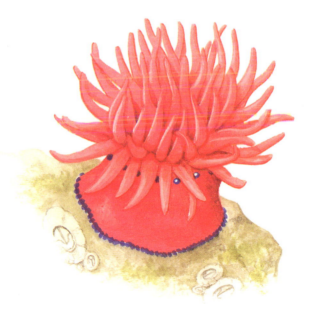

Kingfisher Books

NEW YORK

KINGFISHER BOOKS
Grisewood & Dempsey Inc.
95 Madison Avenue
New York, New York 10016

First American edition 1994
10 9 8 7 6 5 4 3 2 1 (lib. bdg.)
10 9 8 7 6 5 4 3 2 1 (pbk.)

Library of Congress Cataloging-in-Publication Data
Chinery, Michael.
    Questions and answers about seashore animals / by
Michael Chinery; illustrated by Wayne Ford, Mick
Loates, and Mike Taylor. – 1st American ed.
        p. cm.
    Includes index.
    1. Seashore fauna – Miscellanea – Juvenile literature.
[1. Seashore animals.] I. Ford, Wayne, ill. II. Loates,
Mick, ill. III. Taylor, Mike, ill. IV. Title. V. Title:
Seashore animals.
QL122.2.C56 1994
591.909'46 – dc20 93-29428 CIP AC

ISBN 1-85697-981-4 (lib. bdg.)
ISBN 1-85697-965-2 (pbk.)

Series editor: Mike Halson
Series designer: Terry Woodley
Designer: Dave West Children's Books
Illustrators: Norman Michael Fahy (p. 38); Wayne Ford
(pp. 1–3, 12–13, 17, 27, 29, 32–3); Mick Loates/Linden
Artists (pp. 8, 14, 20–21, 28, 34); Myke Taylor/Garden
Studio (pp. 4–7, 9–11, 15–16, 18–19, 22–26, 30–31,
35–37)
Cover illustrations: John Butler
Printed in Hong Kong.

CONTENTS

What is life like on the seashore?

Seashores are not all the same. They vary depending on the kind of rock forming the coast. Hard rocks form rugged headlands and rocky beaches, but softer rocks are more likely to produce sandy bays. The animals of these two kinds of seashores are very different. Rocky shores are great for exploring at low tide because hundreds of different animals cling to the rocks and seaweeds. Animals that live on sandy shores have to burrow into the sand when the tide goes out, and this makes the beach look rather empty.

DO YOU KNOW

The tides that sweep in and out over the beaches twice a day are produced by the Sun and the Moon. The highest tides are when the Sun and Moon are both pulling in the same direction.

Waves are made by the wind blowing over the sea and rippling the surface. The stronger the winds, the higher the waves.

On a rocky shore, seaweeds provide vital food and shelter for many animals. When the tide goes out, most of the animals hide away or fix their shells tightly to the rocks—but where there are rock pools you can watch some seashore creatures moving around in the water.

THE HIGH-WATER MARK

Every time the tide sweeps over the beach it brings with it seaweed and other bits and pieces. This junk stays behind and forms the high-water mark, the highest level reached by the tide before going out. It is a good place to look for small seashore animals.

MANGROVE SWAMPS

Many tropical sea-shores are fringed with small trees called mangroves. These trees all have masses of branching roots, looking like upturned baskets. The roots anchor them in the shifting mud and sand. Mangrove swamps are home to huge numbers of crabs and birds.

Which crab climbs trees?

Robber crabs live on tropical beaches. When they are young they live in the sea, but adults drown if kept underwater for more than a few hours. They feed on dead animals, and can climb trees to get coconuts and other fruit.

Robber crabs use long front claws to climb coconut palms, but it is not true that they throw coconuts to the ground to crack them.

The adult robber crab is about 18 inches long. It has very powerful claws and only four walking legs.

Which fish can walk on mud?

Mudskippers are weird fish that live in coastal swamps in the warmer parts of the world. When the tide goes out they walk and leap over the mud on their armlike front fins. They can even climb trees. They feed on tiny animals in the mud.

The male mudskipper waves the big fin on its back like a flag to attract females.

How is a skimmer's beak special?

Skimmers are well-named birds. They skim over the sea with the lower half of their strange beak in the water ready to scoop up fish and squid. They fish mainly in the evening or at night. The birds shown here are black skimmers from the Atlantic coast of North America. African and Indian skimmers feed mainly in fresh water.

SKIMMER FACTS

● Skimmers are related to gulls. Black skimmers, 20 inches long, are the largest.

● Young skimmers have normal beaks. They pick up their food from the shore.

Skimmers spend the daytime resting on rocks and sandbanks. They can be easily recognized by their oddly shaped beaks.

As soon as the beak touches something in the water it snaps shut. The head is then raised and the prey is swallowed.

The trail of shining bubbles attracts more fish, so the skimmer turns back ready for a second helping.

How does the gray sea eagle catch fish?

The gray sea eagle is a powerful bird of prey living around the coasts of Europe and Asia. It also lives by large lakes and rivers. The eagle scoops fish from the surface with its big talons, but rarely plunges right into the water. Dead sheep also make up part of the eagle's diet in some areas, and it may kill small lambs. The birds build untidy nests in tall trees or on high cliffs. They usually lay two eggs, and the chicks fly when they are about ten weeks old.

DO YOU KNOW

The gray sea eagle is like a pirate. It does not always bother to go fishing itself. It often waits for other birds to fly up with fish and then it chases them until they are exhausted and give up their possessions— just as human pirates did in the past.

Broad wings, about 3 feet across, enable the eagle to carry heavy loads back to its nest.

SURVIVAL WATCH

Gray seas eagles were hunted out of existence in the British Isles 80 years ago, but Norwegian birds taken to Scotland in 1975 are now doing well. More are now being released in Ireland.

The eagle's long toes have sharp spines on them to help the bird grip the fish securely as it flies.

How do sea urchins use their spines?

Sea urchins look like pincushions with the points sticking outward. These spines protect the urchins and help them to walk and dig in the sand. Long water-filled suckers also help with movement. There is a thin shell just under the skin. Most sea urchins feed on seaweeds, which they scrape from the rocks using tough jaws on their underside. Others feed on debris that they collect with their suckers. Some urchins have very short spines that look more like fur. The spines all fall off when the animals die.

Sea urchins start life as tiny swimming larvae like the one shown below. After a while the larvae lose the ability to swim and they sink down to live on the seabed.

CIDARIS

Cidaris walks over the seabed on its stout spines, which are up to 6 inches long. They are purple at first but turn gray as they age.

The shells of edible sea urchins, up to 6 inches across, make good ornaments. A spine was attached to each pimple in life.

Gulls and other sea-birds often attack rock urchins to get at the soft flesh. The broken shells are often seen on the shore.

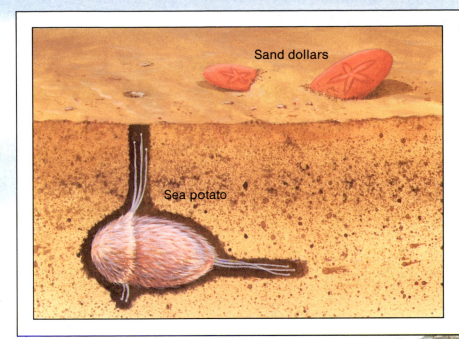

Sand dollars

Sea potato

UNUSUAL URCHINS

Sand dollars are flat, cookie-shaped urchins with short, furlike spines. They eat scraps of food as they plow through the sand. Sea potatoes burrow in the sand. Some of their long suckers collect food, and others reach the surface to allow the urchin to breathe.

Rock urchins live in rock pools. They hide themselves with bits of broken shells and seaweed, held on by their suckers.

 URCHIN FACTS

● There are about 600 kinds of sea urchins, ranging from $\frac{1}{2}$ inch to 18 inches in diameter, including their spines.

● The spines of some sea urchins can cause painful wounds if you step on them.

Edible sea urchins normally live below the low-water mark or in rock pools. The soft inner parts are good to eat.

How do mussels stick to rocks?

Deep blue mussel shells cover the rocks on many seashores. The mussels are anchored by tough threads and they never need to move. They feed by straining tiny scraps of food from the water brought in by the tide.

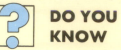 **DO YOU KNOW**

Many of the mussels we eat come from mussel farms. The mussels grow in long socklike nets that hang in the water. Always surrounded by water and plenty of food, the mussels grow very quickly.

These openings are used to suck in food and water and pump the water out again.

Which shellfish holds treasure?

Oysters are shellfish whose shells are firmly cemented to underwater rocks. They feed by straining food particles from the water. People harvest tons of them each year for food. Oysters are also famous for their pearls, which are used in jewelry.

The upper half of the oyster's crinkly shell is flat and sits on the saucer-shaped lower half like a lid.

 **DO YOU KNOW**

A pearl is produced when a sand grain gets inside the shell and irritates the oyster's skin. The oyster covers the sand with layers of smooth, shiny material and this becomes the pearl.

Pearl

What kind of animal is a limpet?

Limpets are sea snails that live on rocky shores. When the tide comes in they glide over the rocks to graze on the seaweeds. When the tide goes out each limpet returns to its own spot and settles down to rest.

Circular marks show where limpets once lived and their hard shells wore grooves in the rocks.

When out of the water at low tide, the limpet uses its strong muscles to pull the shell tight against the rock. It is extremely hard to pull the animal off.

Which limpet resembles a shoe?

The slipper limpet gets its name because its shell looks rather like a slipper. It is a sea snail, but it does not move around. It fixes itself to stones or other shells around the low-water mark and feeds by filtering tiny food particles from the water.

? DO YOU KNOW

Young slipper limpets are all males, but they turn into females as they get older.

Slipper limpets ruin oyster beds by settling on the oysters and stopping them feeding.

Slipper limpets form chains or clusters as big as a man's fist. The smallest and youngest ones in the group are all males.

Why do puffins look funny?

The puffin is famous for its big, colorful beak and its comical, clownlike walk. It looks a bit like a penguin when walking but, unlike penguins, it can also fly. Puffins eat fish and often go far out to sea in the winter. In the summer they breed on the coasts of the North Atlantic and on islands in the Arctic Ocean.

Puffins nest in holes on the tops of cliffs. They often use old rabbit burrows. Females lay just one egg as a rule.

Puffins feed mainly on sand lances. They can carry up to 30 of these slender fish in their big beaks at one time.

The puffin uses its broad webbed feet to change direction and slow itself down when it is flying.

A puffin is about 8 inches high. It flies well, although its plump body looks too heavy for its narrow wings.

How do fanworms gather food?

Vast numbers of worms live on the seashore. They hide under the sand when the tide goes out, but wading birds still find them and eat them. The worms come out to feed when the tide comes in. Many are called fanworms. Instead of hunting, these worms sit still and strain food from the water with fans of feathery tentacles. Most fanworms live in tubes, which often stick out of the sand when the tide is out.

The sand mason (below) glues sand and broken shells together to build a tube. Sabella (on the right) uses much finer sand grains for its tube.

Sabella

Sand-mason

The lugworm spends its entire life in a U-shaped burrow. It sucks mud in through its mouth and passes it out at the other end to form worm casts. The worm digests any scraps of food that it sucks in with the mud.

Lugworm tunnel

Cast

Plug

Serpula fixes its chalky tube to a rock. It hides in its tube when the tide goes out and closes the entrance with a special plug-shaped tentacle.

Honeycomb worms live in large colonies. Their clusters of sandy tubes are fixed to rocks—often in rock pools—and look just like honeycombs.

23

Why do wading birds have long beaks?

Huge flocks of long-legged wading birds visit the seashores, especially in the winter. They come to feed on the millions of worms, shellfish, and shrimplike creatures that live in the sand, mud, and shallow water along the shore. Many of these birds have very long beaks, with which they feel for prey in the sand or mud. Others catch their food by sweeping their beaks through the water. Many waders are great travelers. They spend the summer in the far north and then fly south to spend the winter by the sea.

The black-winged stilt's extremely long, thin legs enable it to wade in deeper water than other waders to find its food.

The avocet searches for crustaceans in the shallows by sweeping its slightly upturned beak from side to side through the water.

The long beaks of some waders enable them to find food deep in the mud. Short-beaked waders find food near the surface.

Despite their name, oystercatchers do not catch oysters. Cockles and mussels are their favorite foods.

The spoonbill has a spoon-shaped beak, which it sweeps through the water to catch shrimps and other small animals.

The redshank scampers over the shore and sweeps its thin beak from side to side through the sand or mud to find food.

The ringed plover usually nests on the shore, where its spotted eggs are well camouflaged among the sand and shingle.

The turnstone gets its name because it uses its beak to turn over stones and other objects while it is searching for food.

What is the spiny lobster's other name?

Spiny lobsters, or crayfish, live in rocky places—usually below low-tide level. Up to 18 inches long, they are a popular food. They lack the big pincers of true lobsters.

The spiny lobster has no big claws. It defends itself by lashing out with its long, spiny antennae.

How do horseshoe crabs look for food?

Horseshoe crabs, or king crabs, live on sandy beaches in the warmer parts of the world. They can swim on their backs, but spend most of their time digging in the sand in search of worms and other small animals.

 **HORSESHOE CRAB FACTS**

● Horseshoe crabs are about 2 feet long.

● The horseshoe crab is not really a crab. It is more closely related to land-dwelling spiders and scorpions.

The spiky tail pushes the animal along, and also turns it the right way up if it is over-turned by waves.

How do shrimps and prawns swim?

Shrimps and prawns are related to crabs, but they are much slimmer and usually swim well. They have five pairs of legs, with pincers on the front ones and some-times on others as well. The back half of the body carries small, feathery limbs that are used as paddles when swimming. The tail fan can be opened out and used as a flipper.

These animals eat whatever they can find on the seabed. We eat a lot of them ourselves. Live ones are mostly brown, but they turn pink when cooked.

Chameleon prawns live in rock pools, but they are hard to see because they change color to match their backgrounds—just like real chameleons. They are sand-colored on sand, but green or brown if crawling on seaweed.

The common prawn is up to 4 inches long and can be easily recog-nized by the pointed, sawlike ridge on the top of its head.

Prawns like rocky areas and you can often see them walking or swimming in rock pools. They use the front two pairs of legs, which have little pincers on them, to pick up scraps of food.

The female prawn glues more than 2,000 eggs to her swimming legs and carries them until they hatch a few weeks later.

The Norway lobster likes muddy areas and does not often come to the shore. It uses its big pincers for defense and collects food with the smaller ones. The Norway lobster's flesh is called scampi.

The Norway lobster is up to 6 inches long and does not swim. Its rather flat body is designed for crawling over sand and mud.

The skeleton shrimp, or ghost shrimp, is not a real shrimp at all. It clings to seaweed and grabs small animals with its claws.

The common shrimp looks like a prawn, but it has no toothed ridge on its head and its front legs are much stouter. The shrimp hides in the sand by day and hunts for animal food at night.

Why are seashore animals in danger?

Many seashores are littered with plastic bottles and ropes and other trash, but the most serious problem is oil. Huge ships carry oil across the oceans, and if there is an accident thousands of tons of oil may leak into the sea. Tides wash the oil onto the shore and, as well as spoiling the beaches for swimming, it destroys the seashore plants and animals. We can clean a sandy beach quite quickly, but nature needs many years to clean the rocks and replace the lost seaweeds and animal life.

SAVING SEABIRDS

The worst casualties of oil spills are puffins and other seabirds that have to dive through the oil to catch their fish. Covered with the slimy oil, they die if they get no help. Luckily, we can clean them with special detergents or soap. As long as the birds have not swallowed too much oil they will survive. They are kept in captivity until their feathers have regained their natural water-proofing—and then they are released.

Oil leaking from a damaged tanker forms a thick black sheet on the surface of the water. Detergents help to break this up, while people and machines struggle to remove the sticky oil from the beach.

Useful words

Antenna   One of the feelers of crabs and their relatives that help the animals to pick up smells and to find their way around.

Bivalve   The name given to any of the seashells, such as cockles and mussels, that are in two parts with a hinge along one edge.

Camouflage   The way in which animals avoid the attention of their enemies by resembling their surroundings or blending in with them. The animals are then not easy to recognize.

Coast   The edge of the land, where it meets the sea.

Crustacean   Any member of the crab and lobster group of animals—hard-shelled creatures with lots of legs.

Eurasia   The name given to the large land mass that consists of the continents of Europe and Asia.

Fin   Any of the limbs or other flaps that fish use for swimming.

Gill   The breathing organ of fish, crustaceans, and many other water-dwelling animals. It takes life-giving oxygen from the water flowing over it.

High-water mark   The line of debris left on the shore at high-tide level.

Larva   The name given to a young animal, particularly a crustacean or an insect, that is noticeably different in shape from the adult.

Marine   Concerning the sea.

Mollusk   Any animal of the group containing slugs, snails, and bivalves. Mollusks have soft bodies and no legs, and most are enclosed in a hard shell.

Scavenger   An animal that feeds mainly on dead matter—especially one that clears up the remains of another animal's meal.

Shellfish   The name given to various hard-shelled sea creatures, especially cockles and mussels and their relatives. Crabs and other crustaceans are also commonly known as shellfish.

Shingle   Coarse gravel and pebbles, up to about 2 inches across, found on the upper parts of the seashore.

Siphon   A tube through which many mollusks suck water into their bodies for breathing and feeding. Many have a second siphon for pumping the water out again.

Tentacle   A soft, fingerlike projection that is found near the mouth of many animals, including sea anemones. Tentacles are normally used for catching food.

Tide   The regular rise and fall of sea level, which floods and then uncovers the seashore twice every day.

Tropical   To do with the tropics—the warm areas of the world on each side of the equator.

Wader   The name given to various long-legged birds that feed on marshland and in shallow water at the edge of the sea

Index

A
antenna 12, 35, 39
avocet 24

B
barnacle 27
bird of prey 17
bivalve 32, 39
black skimmer 16
black-headed gull 6
black-winged stilt 24
bristleworm 14

C
camouflage 25, 39
chameleon prawn 36
Cidaris 18
clown fish 11
coast 39
cockle 25, 32, 39
common prawn 36
common shrimp 37
cone shell 33
cormorant 29
crab 12-13, 14, 15, 26, 27, 30,
    35, 36, 39
crayfish 35
crustacean 29, 39

D
dahlia anemone 11

E
edible crab 12, 13
edible sea urchin 18, 19
Eurasia 6, 17, 39

F
fairy penguin 31
fanworm 23
fiddler crab 26
fin 15, 28, 39

G
Galapagos penguin 31
ghost crab 13
giant clam 33
gill 34, 39
goby 28
gray sea eagle 17
gray sea slug 34
great black-backed gull 6
guanay cormorant 29
guillemot 29

H
hermit crab 14
herring gull 7
high-water mark 5, 6, 39
honeycomb worm 23
horseshoe crab 35

J
jackass penguin 31
Japanese spider crab 12

K
king crab 35

L
larva 13, 18, 39
limpet 21
lobster 35, 37, 39
lugworm 23

M
mangrove 5, 13, 30
mangrove crab 13
marine 9, 39
marine iguana 9
masked crab 12
mollusk 32, 39
mudskipper 15
murex 33
mussel 8, 13, 20, 25, 39

N
Norway lobster 37

O
oyster 20
oyster bed 21
oystercatcher 25

P
pearl 20
piddock 27
plumose anemone 10
prawn 36-7
puffin 22, 38

Q
queen conch 33

R
red beadlet anemone 11
redshank 25

ringed plover 25
robber crab 15
rock urchin 18

S
Sabella 23
sand dollar 19
sand lance 22
sand-mason 23
scallop 33
scampi 36-7
scarlet ibis 30
scavenger 6, 39
sea anemone 10-11, 14, 34, 39
sea lemon 34
sea potato 19
sea slug 34
sea snail 14, 21, 32, 33, 34
sea urchin 18-19
seagull 6-7
seashell 27, 32-3, 39
Serpula 23
shellfish 20, 24, 39
shingle 15, 39
shore crab 12
shrimp 14, 25, 28, 36-7
siphon 27, 32, 39
skeleton shrimp 37
skimmer 16
slipper limpet 21
snakelocks anemone 11
spiny lobster 35
spoonbill 25
starfish 8
sting 10, 11, 14, 34

T
tellin 32
tentacle 10, 11, 23, 39
tide 4, 5, 39
tiger cowrie 32
tropical 5, 15, 26, 30, 33, 39
turnstone 25

V
velvet crab 12

W
wader 25, 39
wading bird 23, 24-5
weever fish 28